FAILURES THAT FUELED TRANSPORTATION

FANTASTIC FAILURES
From Flops to Fortune

MARTIN GITLIN

45TH PARALLEL PRESS

Published in the United States of America by Cherry Lake Publishing Group
Ann Arbor, Michigan
www.cherrylakepublishing.com

Reading Adviser: Beth Walker Gambro, MS, Ed., Reading Consultant, Yorkville, IL
Series Adviser: Virginia Loh-Hagan
Book Designer: Frame25 Productions

Photo Credits: © Dmitry Molchanov/Shutterstock, cover, title page; © OlegRi/Shutterstock, 4; © Gorodenkoff/ Shutterstock, 5; Unattributed, Public domain, via Wikimedia Commons, 7; © Tudoran Andrei, 8; The Library of Congress, No restrictions, via Wikimedia Commons, 9; Mariordo (Mario Roberto Durán Ortiz), CC BY-SA 4.0 via Wikimedia Commons, 10; Attributed to Wilbur and/or Orville Wright., Public domain, via Wikimedia Commons, 11; © muratart/Shutterstock, 12; © Rawpixel.com/Shutterstock, 15; © ToKa74/Shutterstock, 16; Le Petit Journal Supplément du Dimanche, Public domain, via Wikimedia Commons, 17; © Daisy Daisy/Shutterstock, 18; Luz28, CC0, via Wikimedia Commons, 19; Hartsook, photographer., Public domain, via Wikimedia Commons, 20; Henry Perronet Briggs, Public domain, via Wikimedia Commons, 23; E. J. Claghorn, Public domain, via Wikimedia Commons, 24; Marvin Dement Boland, Public domain, via Wikimedia Commons, 25; © Molotok289/Shutterstock, 26; National Institute of Standards and Technology, Public domain, via Wikimedia Commons, 27; © Jean Faucett/ Shutterstock, 28; © Branislav Nenin/Shutterstock, 29; Harris & Ewing, photographer, Public domain, via Wikimedia Commons, 32

45th Parallel Press is an imprint of Cherry Lake Publishing Group.

Library of Congress Cataloging-in-Publication Data has been filed and is available at catalog.loc.gov

Cherry Lake Publishing would like to acknowledge the work of the Partnership for 21st Century Learning, a network of Battelle for Kids. Please visit Battelle for Kids online for more information.

Printed in the United States of America

Note from publisher: Websites change regularly, and their future contents are outside of our control. Supervise children when conducting any recommended online searches for extended learning opportunities.

Contents

INTRODUCTION

"If at first you don't succeed, try, try again." This is an old saying. It's been said a lot. It's a great tip. Failure is part of life. It's not bad. It can have good results. People must not let failure defeat them. They should keep trying. Failing can lead to success.

People in transportation help people. They move people from one place to another. They make the world an easier place to travel. They try out things. They know about failing. They learn from their mistakes. They have ideas.

But not all ideas work. Some ideas **flop**. *Flop* means to fail. Ideas may not work as planned. Successful people don't give up. They solve problems. They find other uses for flops. They turn flops into fortunes.

The transportation world has many examples. Many great products started as failures. These failures worked out. They made life easier. They helped people at work. They helped people at home.

Successful inventors show **persistence**. Persisting means not quitting. Their hard work paid off. That is a lesson everyone can learn.

CHAPTER 1

Repeated Failures of Flying Machines

....

Airplanes have been flying for more than 100 years. They don't get much attention anymore. Most folks rarely think about them. They see planes zoom through the sky. Planes are no longer a marvel. But they weren't always common. The idea of flying once seemed impossible.

Flying had been a dream. People long ago saw birds fly. They wondered if humans could do the same. Brothers Wilbur and Orville Wright dreamed of flying. They grew up in Dayton, Ohio.

The brothers opened a bike business together. But they were more interested in flying. They wanted to build flying machines. Other flying machines had been built. People around the world had tried. They all flopped. The Wright brothers studied hard. They learned from others' failures.

Some flying machines had reached the air. But the pilots couldn't control them. The Wright brothers had to figure out why. They looked at how birds fly. They studied birds' wings.

Brothers Orville Wright (1871-1948) and Wilbur Wright (1867-1912)

They wrote to Octave Chanute. Chanute was an engineer. He was born in France. He had moved to the United States at age 16. He had helped build flying machines. He gave the Wright brothers tips.

The brothers had to practice. They went to Kitty Hawk in North Carolina. It's on the Atlantic Ocean. It had strong winds. Strong winds would help planes fly. Kitty Hawk also had sandy beaches. These beaches would ensure soft landings.

The Wright brothers designed a plane. They had to discover how to keep it in the air. They tested different wing designs. One after another failed. Their planes stayed in the air only a short time. Then they'd crash. But the Wright brothers kept trying.

They returned to Dayton. Then they went back to Kitty Hawk. They tried a bigger plane design. Their new design had bigger wings. It stayed up for nearly 400 feet (121.9 meters). That's when the pilot lost control.

The Wright brothers kept going. They kept trying. They kept failing. They built a new plane in 1902. This new plane had longer wings. The wings were 16 feet (4.9 m) long. They weighed 112 pounds (50.8 kilograms).

The Wright brothers tested the plane. Some things worked. Some things didn't. The brothers moved parts around. They made it easier to fly.

Wilbur hopped in. He took off. His flight covered 622 feet (189.6 m). It lasted 26 seconds.

The next goal was a flight powered by gas. That meant adding a motor. The plane couldn't weigh more than 180 pounds (81.6 kg). Soon the new design was ready. It was December 17, 1903. It was a cold day in Kitty Hawk. A strong wind was blowing. The weather was dangerous for flight. But the brothers didn't want to wait. They decided to fly close to the ground. A crash from high in the sky would be bad. It could kill the pilot.

The plane took off. Orville flew it. He was 10 feet (3 m) from the ground. He stayed up for 12 seconds. The flight was a big success. The brothers wanted to do better. They kept trying. They took turns flying. They did this for hours. Wilbur soared 852 feet (259.7 m). He stayed in flight for 59 seconds.

The airplane had been invented. Better designs made them faster. Planes became safer. They could stay up for hours. They're among the greatest inventions ever. People can be across the globe in hours. They just have to hop on a plane. Today's flying machines are so easy to use. The Wright brothers made flight possible.

FLOPPED!
The Ford Edsel

It was September 4, 1957. The Ford Motor Company makes cars. Its workers were excited. They had designed a new car. It was being launched. It was called the Edsel. Ford had been promoting the Edsel. It had spent a year teasing buyers. It made 18 different models. It claimed that the Edsel was the car of the future. But there was one problem. Ford had polled car shoppers. It asked people what they wanted. Then it ignored the answers. The Edsel flopped. It was too expensive. It didn't run well. Most people didn't like how it looked. Ford lost $250 million. Companies should listen to their buyers.

CHAPTER 2

The Accidental Discovery of Safety Glass

....

Safety is the most important feature for a car. It's critical for any mode of transportation. People travel. They need to feel safe. They don't want to crash. They don't want to die.

Most people don't think about car windows. They assume these windows are safe. Car windows are strong. They might crack when hit by an object. But they rarely break. People can thank Edouard Benedictus for that.

Benedictus was French. He was a scientist. But he was also creative. He was an artist. He was a writer. He wrote music. These skills helped him think outside the box. They helped him see old problems in new ways. In 1903, he became an inventor. But he didn't know it.

It all started when he was climbing a ladder. He hit a shelf. He knocked off an empty glass **flask**. Flasks are containers. They hold **liquids**. Liquids are watery substances. Benedictus heard the glass shatter. But the flask still held its shape. The glass was cracked. But the glass pieces stayed together.

That seemed odd. Benedictus wondered why. He saw something special in the flask. He asked a friend about it. The flask contained cellulose nitrate. This is a liquid plastic.

Benedictus remained curious. He read a newspaper article. The article was about driving cars in Paris. The new cars were dangerous. Many accidents happened. Drivers got hurt. They were hit by broken windshield glass. This made Benedictus think.

Benedictus remembered the flask. He thought about windshields. Windshields could be safer. They could be coated with the special liquid. This would stop glass bits from flying.

Benedictus went to work. He spent the next day testing. He bound 2 sheets of glass together outside a clear plastic. He had invented safety glass. He called it triplex. He got a **patent** 6 years later. Patents are legal rights. They protect inventors' ideas.

Safety glass made windshields safer. But one problem remained. It cost too much money to make. Some car companies didn't want to use it. They didn't want to spend the money.

Safety glass was rarely used until World War I (1914–1918). The glass was first used for gas masks. It was used for the lenses. These gas masks were worn by soldiers. They protected them against poison gas.

The glass was easy to make. New designs made them cheaper. Henry Ford was a U.S. businessman. He owned a car company. He valued safety. He placed safety glass in some Ford cars. By 1929, safety glass was in all of Ford's cars. Other car companies followed. Now all cars use safety glass.

Driving has become much safer. Benedictus and his flask have saved many lives.

Henry Ford (1863-1947)

FLOPPED!
The DeLorean

John DeLorean made cars. He had an idea. He wanted to make a unique car. He thought buyers would love it. It was 1975. DeLorean opened a car factory in Ireland. He built a car. The car cost $150 million to build. DeLorean named the car after himself. He called it the DeLorean. He created only 9,000 models. They were odd. The doors opened like airplane wings. They were made of stainless steel. That way, they could be easily fixed. The DeLorean hit the market in 1981. It got strong reviews from car **critics**. Critics review and judge things. They liked the DeLorean's design. They thought it was fun. Buyers didn't care. The DeLorean failed. Few people bought it. It was among the biggest flops in car history. But the DeLorean gained fame in film. It was shown in the 1985 movie *Back to the Future*. In the movie, it was a time machine.

CHAPTER 3

The Repeated Rejection of Seat Belts

··

It's a habit for everyone. It's also the law in most U.S. states. People get into a car. They reach across their chests. They pull down the seat belt. They click it in. Most of us do this without thinking. This practice has saved many lives. But seat belts weren't used for many years. They were invented before the first cars were made. Yet they weren't placed in the early models.

George Cayley invented the first seat belt. Cayley was an inventor from England. He loved the idea of flight.

He built a flying machine in 1804. His invention was the first **manned glider**. Manned means controlled by a human. Gliders are special aircraft. They don't have engines. Cayley was just getting started. In 1853, he made a much bigger glider. He knew it was dangerous to fly. So he made a seat belt. The seat belt would hold the pilot in place. His invention worked. His first test flight crashed. But the pilot survived. That is because he wore his seat belt.

Sir George Cayley (1773-1857)

The seat belt came to New York City. This happened in 1885. Edward Claghorn got a patent. Claghorn's invention was simple. It was a strap held tight by hooks. It kept riders safe in horse-drawn carriages.

That was not enough to make seat belts popular. Neither was their first use in car racing. In 1922, the seat belt was first used in racing. This was at the Indy 500. This famous car race is held in Indianapolis, Indiana.

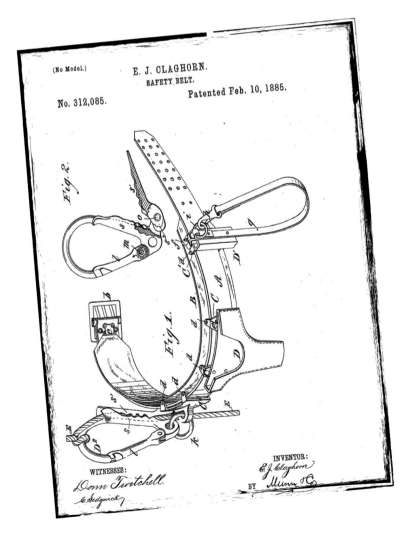

Barney Oldfield (1878-1946)

Driver Barney Oldfield was the first to use a seat belt. He was the first to drive 60 miles (96.6 kilometers) per hour. Today, Indy 500 drivers reach 235 miles (378.2 km) per hour. Oldfield had a dangerous job. Race car drivers crash. They get thrown from their cars. They get hurt. Some get killed. Oldfield wanted to protect himself. He wanted a seat belt. He had one designed.

People still had the wrong idea about seat belts. Some thought they were unsafe. They felt it was safer to be thrown from a car. They feared being trapped. They thought it would be hard to escape a crashed car. Car makers thought it was a bad idea too. They didn't want buyers to think cars were unsafe.

People kept rejecting seat belts. This started to change in 1959. Nils Bohlin was a Swiss engineer. He invented a new model. His belt didn't just go over the lap. It also held the upper body in place. That was the most important seat belt **innovation** ever. An innovation is a new idea or process. It saved lives.

Wisconsin took the lead among U.S. states. It required seat belts in all cars in 1961. But the law was only for front seats. And no law forced people to wear them.

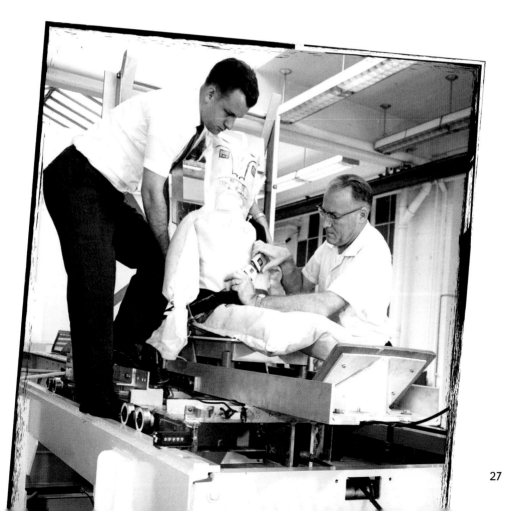

Too many people without seat belts were getting hurt. Many died. This could be prevented. Wearing seat belts was an easy solution. The U.S. government finally acted in 1968. It required seat belts to be in all new cars. They had to secure both the lap and shoulder. But there was still no law about wearing them. Some people didn't like them. They felt held back by seat belts.

That changed in 1984. New York passed a law. It forced people to wear seat belts. It was only for riders in the front seat. But those older than age 16 had to wear one in the back seat. Other states followed. All states but one now require people to use seat belts. That state is New Hampshire.

Today, most people know seat belts are important. Seat belts make a difference. They save about 15,000 lives every year.

SUCCESS STORY!
Goodyear Tires

Goodyear is a famous tire company. It's based in Akron, Ohio. Its founder was Charles Goodyear. Goodyear had an accident in 1839. He dropped some rubber on a hot stove. The stove had sulfur on it. Sulfur is a **chemical** element. Chemical means related to chemistry. Goodyear watched what happened. He was surprised. He found that the rubber became harder. The rubber was stronger than before. His discovery changed the world. It became known as vulcanized rubber. Goodyear uses it to make car tires. Vulcanized rubber is used to make other products. Examples are hockey pucks and rubber boots.

LEARN MORE

Books

Barr, Catherine, and Steve Williams. *The Story of Inventions: A First Book about World-Changing Discoveries.* London: Frances Lincoln Children's Books, 2020.

Jones, Charlotte Foltz. *Mistakes That Worked: The World's Familiar Inventions and How They Came to Be.* New York: Delacorte Press, 2016.

Whipple, Annette. *The Story of the Wright Brothers: A Biography Book for New Readers.* Berkeley, CA: Rockridge Press, 2020.

Websites

With an adult, explore more online with these suggested searches.

"Inventions," Kids Discover

"Invention Process," Inventive Kids

"Wright Brothers Facts for Kids," Kiddle

GLOSSARY

chemical (KEH-mih-kuhl) having to do with the science of chemistry

critics (KRIH-tiks) people who judge something

flask (FLASK) a rounded bottle with a narrow neck used for holding liquids

flop (FLAHP) to fail

glider (GLYE-der) unique aircraft that does not use an engine to fly

innovation (ih-nuh-VAY-shuhn) a new idea, method, or product

liquids (LIH-kwuhdz) watery substances that flow freely but have a constant volume

manned (MAND) carrying or operated by humans or a crew

patent (PA-tuhnt) a government document allowing someone the sole right to make and sell an invention

persistence (per-SIH-stuhns) the will to keep trying after first failing or experiencing challenges

INDEX

ABOUT THE AUTHOR

Martin Gitlin is an educational book author based in Connecticut. He won more than 45 awards as a newspaper sportswriter from 1991 to 2002. Included was a first-place award from the Associated Press for his coverage of the 1995 World Series. He has had more than 200 books published since 2006. Most of them were written for students.